MOMENTS WITH
GRANDMA
MOOSE

GRANDMA MOOSE

ISBN 978-1-0980-0387-6 (paperback)
ISBN 978-1-0980-0388-3 (digital)

Christian Faith Publishing, Inc.
832 Park Avenue
Meadville, PA 16335
www.christianfaithpublishing.com

Printed in the United States of America

This book is dedicated to their granddaughters Emily & Carrie
and their great granddaughters Audrey, Sabrina, & Emma Rose.
A little walk into the past.

Freedom

My spirit is in a constant state of gratitude,
As I hold my pen as if it were my favorite food.
A miracle that I don't quite understand,
But feel it holds a message ever so grand.

Words form and flow, I know not how.
Only do they know who is directing just now.
I, a servant, only hold the pen.
At what point this began, I know not when.

But I feel it's special...just not for me to know.
One day perhaps the answer will come as winds blow.
A servant doesn't question...it's not our place.
The picture isn't clear...it's like looking through fine lace.

The answer is out beyond us at this time.
It's all wrapped up in the words that rhyme.
I am but a humble messenger, at best.
With these wonderful, heartfelt words I'm blessed.

When I simply said, "Send me, send me."
He gave me a pen and set me free.

A Light in the Window

Remember Mom saying "I'll keep a light in the window?"
You just looked for its soft, warming glow
That marked your home, so you found your way back.
Wouldn't want you to travel on the wrong track.

"Home is where the heart is," I've heard it said.
Or maybe you just follow that fragrance of Mom baking bread.
We will all be waiting...just look for the light.
Home is where a soul rests from every troublesome plight.

Our Father has a light on in his heavenly window for us, too...
Always on—sun, moon, or stars—just waiting for you.
Earth is a big place, so easy to lose your way,
So just look toward his sky...away from the fray.

God's light is constant, it never, ever goes out.
He lived here once and knows what trouble is all about.
Take a moment and check out the glow for direction.
It will always help you to make a blessed selection.

Mine?

Have I buried the words from my pen in the sand?
Have I failed my Maker that guides me with his hand?

Am I afraid of the world, I can't seem to move ahead?
After all, those rhyming words were never really in my head.

But they were from the Creator of all things on earth.
He alone joined the words and gave them birth.

I'm just a servant in this thought-sharing task.
Such an honor, Father, for more I could not ask.

We shall tell your name from sea to sea.
To you, Father, I will always say, "Send me, send me."

I await for a door to open and a light to shine
Because I'm so sure these messages are not really mine.

Music for the Soul

Notes trickle down like a forgotten rain,
Leaving a lasting, lilting melody in your brain.
It tells a story often of your own making,
While you rock the baby or do the baking.

It soothes the moment…calms the soul,
And in your heart's sad part, it fills that hole.
Music…always words add to the meaning,
Giving the field of notes a total gleaning.

It pulls from your soul a precious memory nearly lost
Or reminds you of a forgotten path once crossed.
Music soothes hurt feelings and gives them a rest.
Makes you, once again, comfortable in your own little nest.

I've got to go now…my music just stopped playing,
And I've forgotten what I would next be saying.

| GRANDMA MOOSE

Then I'll See

When you think you can't...you will,
Take a moment and just sit still,
Reach back into your center, into your heart,
Go to that little spot where love had its start.

Throw off the feelings of fatigue and sadness,
Exchange them with the Father...he holds all gladness,
He understands your anxiety and sees all your fears,
And knows all you have right now are your tears.

He hung on a cross and knows desperate need,
He hears your words before you even begin to plead,
He is your core. You'll walk on water...he is your center,
Giving you courage...he is your forever mentor.

The sun will rise and the dark clouds melt,
He will help you forget all the depression you felt,
With our spirit renewed, we can get on with the show,
How that can happen, I really don't know.

It's a miracle, for sure...and it happens to me,
Someday my eyes will close, only then will I see.

Winners

Mommy, is Jesus here with us right now?
Does he know every time I hurt myself and say "Ow?"
Can he really walk on a cloud in the sky,
And can he help me when I'm afraid and will cry?

Mom, is Grandpa with him on a rainbow somewhere?
Gramps always said to check with Jesus, he was always fair.
I bet Grandpa asked Jesus how those stars stay so shiny.
Maybe he would know, too, why our little sister is so whiny!

When I get big, I'll be smart and know a lot more,
Even how to pick the sweetest candy in the store.
I bet Jesus knows about that, too…the good stuff, I mean.
You know we share a favorite color and that would be green.

He uses it a lot…all over—grass and the trees
And all the flowers that give honey to the bees.
Seems like he's got most things all figured out.
I know, Mom, you ask him a lot what life is all about.

RANDMA MOOSE

I wonder, is he why we call all men our brother,
Even though we don't exactly look like each other?
Can I go play now before it's time for dinner?
And, Mom, this talk of ours, it was a real winner!

PS: Hope you've enjoyed a
winner lately, too!

Homer...a Bear

Made by hands with limited skill,
Built for hands to play...a child's arms to fill.
Occasionally getting boo-boos, cuts, and scars
And looking like the survivor of many wars.

This is our Homer...such a loveable guy.
No better bear could a fortune ever buy.
He's been slept with, tossed, and spilled upon.
A little bit pudgy...not much for brawn.

His fabric lacks softness, not at all furry.
His look very stoic, without care or a worry.
He's bigger than most, being rather tall,
But he knows size doesn't matter at all.

Big never makes best, of that he is sure.
In fact, that thought seems rather immature.
And Homer has gathered a few years to his name,
Never being interested in status or teddy bear fame.

He serves as a companion to children lost and alone,
And they never judge him on the way he was sewn.
At the moment he's the friend they need so bad,
Even if his worn body is a little bit sad.

He is their port in the storm right now,
To take the worry from a young child's brow.
You're never as lost when you can hug a bear
Because he's right there, all your tears to share.

Homer lives in a shelter for the abused and lost.
Those who, on a sea of conflict, have been tossed.
He sits on a shelf waiting for that one little child
Whose young life has proved to be far from mild.

Their eyes meet and then another story starts.
This is a tale that is all about hearts.
You see, teddy bears help lost little souls to mend,
Putting their sadness and tears to a final end.

Without saying a word, bears have a way
Of giving a child a brand-new bright day.
Now that you've met Homer, remember him well...
Someday you might need a bear, who can tell?

The Cook

As long as a recipe lives, so does the cook.
You will always remember her worn and ragged cookbook.
Dog-eared pages and soils from food being dropped,
And her handwritten notes about the recipes that flopped.
You remember the many annual events by the food prepared,
By the love for each other that was always shared.

You see Grandma growing older through those pages,
Accepting different roles on life's stages.
From eager mother to our beloved granny...always there,
Always with her recipes, but now from her rocking chair,
So this sad-looking book becomes a precious prize.
Never be fooled by its poor condition or small size.

Our granny wrote those ingredients with her own hand,
And when put together, it was always so grand.
This book is almost like a sort of bible to all of us,
When we remember how she was so particular and liked to fuss.
Stir it just so many times and listen for the bell.
And it needs a bit more salt...she could always tell.

The most important thing that Granny left behind
Was a collection of the best loved recipes you will ever find.
But never, my friend, should you ask for a recipe printed out.
Always ask they be handwritten...that's what it's all about.
Yes, as she grows older, the lines may tend to shake.
That's when your heart will surely start to ache.

Her very progression of age is recorded in that small book.
But God knows we will never, ever forget the cook.

Paradise? Where? How?

Paradise is wherever you make it, my friend.
The ingredients are all around, God-given without end.
My chair and music, playing with a loud sound.
And then, a pen and paper are always easy to be found.

There I have it...my paradise, for what more could I ask?
Making our life a blessing, for the Lord is never a task
With everyday full of sweet flowers and birds that sing.
Hey, this paradise is a pretty good thing.

Wherever I roam, God's paradise is right there.
He always has it ready and there for me to share.
When you are surrounded by miracles, what's not to see?
Maybe your faith is lacking...could that be?

Why not look for God's hand in all you see or do?
Just give it a try...it could truly work for you, too!
Well, have a good day. Your paradise is right now.
Maybe you should just relax and let God show you how.

It's Fine

I'm just like a snowflake...one among so many.
We all look much alike, whether a Jack, Jill, or Jennie.

Our life span is short... It goes by really fast,
And there's not much you can do to make it last.

Whether you are part of a snowbank or a snowman,
Just keep up with the rest and do the best you can.

On every flake, God's sun will one day shine.
But not to worry...heaven has a winter and
It will be fine!

A Baby Boy

Here I sit amidst the paper and Christmas frills,
But finding no joy as I wrap a toy that holds thrills.
My concern is for the world that is all around me.
There are many souls who will never a manger see.

No baby, or shepherds, no wise men from afar,
While just now I'm hearing that feared word, war.
Do those folks know the manger child could cause some change?
Having love around would help the world just rearrange.

All things are better when we see with the eyes of love.
Then maybe not missiles but blessings would shower from above.
Children would then not cry out for a parent in their fear.
Nor would we lose the military men and women we hold dear.

What is there to gain? Money...or maybe more power?
I'd rather spend time with a child for one precious hour.
Please, friend, this Christmas night look for that star.
It's been there forever...it has truly come very far.

You might really need the love the manger holds for you.
Maybe it's even just a little overdue!
So, friend, this is Christmas. Oh, what a joy!
For tonight, a king was born...the manger holds a baby boy.

Branches

Please hold me up, Father, lest I fall.
It's only in your presence that I can feel tall,
Then I have the arm of David and a lion's strength.
For you, Abba, I will walk any length.

Should my weakness come on as it does from time to time,
I just sit down and we, sir, compose a rhyme.
My day is brightened and the tunnel's end has light.
It's you, Abba, coming to help. I have you in my sight.

It's woe to those who scoff and do not believe.
I think of all the mercy they will never receive.
But mostly I worry…how blind they seem to be,
To miss all the beauty that is around us to see.

A crooked tree branch, worn and wind tossed.
Yet its rugged beauty is never lost.
A protector of animals from the earth's wild,
Or simply to hold a yard swing for a child.

Offering shade in the heat of a summer day,
Then in autumn becoming a dazzling display.
Breathtaking beauty, God's colors at their best.
This old crooked branch has surely passed the test.

How is your crooked branch doing this fine day?
Think maybe it needs improvement in some way?
Well, I know the best tree man there has ever been.
He even used a tree branch to save us from our sin.

Why Am I Here?

How often man has posed this question through life,
When the days go all wrong and are filled with strife.
Why am I here?

When I don't have the answer to an important question asked
Or the solution to a very difficult task.
Why am I here?

While holding the hand of a loved one dying
And all I can do is stand there crying.
Why am I here?

When the whole world is plummeting into disaster, I know.
There seems no way to turn the evil winds that blow.
Why am I here?

So much poverty and I have so little to give.
How do I offer a lost soul the will to live?
Why am I here?

When the road gets rough and I lose my way,
Just how can I keep going into another new day?
Why am I here?

When a child takes my hand asking to be heard,
Do I try extra hard to find just the right word?
Why am I here?

I'm frightened sometimes in this existence here...
I often feel nearly frozen by my fear.
Why am I here?

Each night I turn to sweet, peaceful sleep,
Asking always that Jesus my soul will keep.
Why am I here?

Then with the rising sun I awake and look around.
Such beautiful miracles, Father, do truly abound.
Why am I here?

That's when I take up my pen and lose track of time
Because that's when Abba and I compose a rhyme.
Why am I here?

So for this minute, this very moment, with all these many words
Forming phrases that land on this paper like lovely birds.
How can I ever again ask, "Why am I here?"
When we hold the words that make my life so dear.

Words

Just give me a moment to gather my thoughts around,
And then a little while of quiet...without a sound.
Then those words and phrases will rearrange and swap places,
And miraculously then will show new faces.

I'll just hold the pen and play tag with my dictionary
Because spelling has always been my worst adversary.
Often Mr. Webster and I go around and around.
Why don't they just spell words the way they sound?

In school I could easily rhyme, but then there was spelling.
My grade in it was never worth the telling.
But words always held a beauty I see so clear,
Then I bring life into focus and make it so dear.

I believe I just see all of my living in rhyme.
So it's with my pen that I will climb.
Higher and higher to a far distant peak,
To the miraculous feelings I always seek.

I'm going to an answered joy, a place close to God.
I just hold the pen and wait for his nod.
For a "job well done" for a "go in peace",
Then for all my errors I find his forgiving release.

Since childhood my favorite words I still lovingly keep.
They will always remain, "Now I lay me down to sleep."

A Christmas Prayer

Father, for a few moments, we are finally alone.
This twenty-fifth of December has really just flown.
I fixed the food, wrapped the gifts, lit the tree.
But, sir, I need now a few minutes just for me.

Over all the years I've enjoyed many lovely Christmas days.
Sometimes I didn't take time to say thanks in the proper ways.
The gifts are not important to me...it's that story about you.
It's about the manger scene, each year it's all so new.

I wonder about the sky as it proudly holds that star,
And I even watch for wise men who travel from afar.
I'm kind of worried, could the shepherds get too cold?
And I long to see his gifts...was that one really gold?

The value doesn't matter, of that I'm quite sure.
Christ chose to be born among those who were poor.
With a crude manger for a bed...humble, indeed,
To have your first bed where animals feed.

Remember, he lived and he died for us, too.
And every day of your life he is there for you.
Why not take a minute each day to think of that manger story
And the child born in such humble glory?

When I get to heaven, I believe I'll find a stable there.
And at that manger I, once more, will offer my Christmas prayer.

No Stall for Humphrey

Humphrey came to Bethlehem one special night
When a star in the heavens was shining so bright.
The trip had been long and he was ready to rest,
But the lodgings here didn't seem quite the best.

His caravan was so small, what was all the fuss?
Their riders had talked long hours...a lot to discuss.
The finest robes were worn, no travel details lacking.
Precious gifts were purchased and they were careful in the packing.

Now Humphrey was a rather pampered camel, indeed,
Accustomed to a nice bed and regular feed.
This stable was not like that...not at all.
There wasn't even an extra animal stall.

And that manger was holding something other than food.
Just where did these people feed this motley brood?
There was a worn-out donkey and a smattering of sheep.
Now where do you suppose Humphrey would have to sleep?

Not with that old cow, he would be definite about that.
He might even have to share a bed with the stable's cat!
And that star was shining on them so bright...
Way too much for sleeping in the middle of the night.

Now Humphrey wondered why they had been in such a rush,
Just to get to this tiny place that held a strange hush.
And there was singing he heard in the distance afar,
Coming from somewhere up there by that bright star.

It was then he saw a baby where his food should be,
And it was surely the most wonderful sight he would ever see.
This child was different... Humphrey wasn't quite sure how,
But he suddenly bent his legs and did an awkward camel bow.

Did everyone here know this was one great event?
Humphrey was sure of it...he just didn't know what it meant.
Those shabby animals were looking in the child's direction.
Their eyes were filled with love and adoring affection.

Then his people brought their gifts of gold, frankincense, and
    myrrh.
Just what a baby did with those, he wasn't really sure.
Humphrey wanted to give a gift to this child, too!
Maybe his old saddle blanket…it was a pretty blue.

So with his hoof he pushed it slowly toward the manger.
It could be a bit of warmth for this little stranger.
He would know who it was from…somehow, he'd know.
Oh, how Humphrey wished he could see this baby grow.

This child would do special things, change lives, give strength.
The stretch of his power would have great length.
Tonight, Humphrey was blessed to be here and see it all,
And he was ever so happy to share a stall.

Listen

Ever think about all the sounds we are privileged to hear?
Some so loud and noisy, they need not be too near.
A crashing wave at sea, or a lightning bolt from the sky,
Or the sounds so precious and soft you just want to cry.
A baby's breath or the tiny secret giggle of a small child,
Those sweet little people that are yet undefiled.

Have you ever heard a single leaf as it falls from God's trees
In the soft soundless early morning breeze?
And as quiet as a mouse, I've heard that said,
But there is a sound I anticipate with some dread.
Some of what I hear doesn't always sit well with me,
And that can also be said for things I often see.

I know that all men differ from time to time.
But often, deeds are so wrong, we then call them crime.
I don't understand this cruel side of life.
There seems no joy in bringing others strife.
Kindness gives happiness to both the giver and receiver.
A handshake can be an instant tension reliever.

I like to sit and listen to birds chirping together.
I'm pretty sure the conversation is all about the weather
Or maybe the new nest in the elm tree down the street.
I can't be sure since they all speak with a tweet.
But just hearing them gives my soul such a lift,
Just another sound God gives us as a daily gift.

Please take a little time to listen for all the
Earth's sound.
Even when you can't understand the language...
The message is profound.

Sense of Humor

I embrace my life with gusto today.
I know all the problems, but it's still okay.
I'm walking and talking within reason,
And I choose to enjoy this great winter season.

It might have fog, snow, and ice in that order.
Not weather I'd recommend for any skateboarder.
But here I am, Lord...dare I say, "Send me. Send me?"
That, at times, has gotten me into some deep, rough sea.

Yet I know you're right there helping me to stay afloat
Because I've never been really good at handling a boat.
I know you will give me a challenge head on,
But you'll be right there...you are never ever gone.

There have been those times I've failed the test.
Try as I might, I just didn't do my best.
I'm ashamed of my actions...after all, you died for me.
So today, Abba, could we start over again?...you'll see.

I'll do your will whatever I can do.
Just remember, sir, I can't walk on the water like you.

PS: I wrote this poem knowing it is a fact, not a rumor,
That our blessed shepherd has a great
sense of humor.

Memories

The music box has lost its spin...the melody fades away.
But not to worry, we will surely hear it yet another day.
Its notes are tucked in our heart and soul...just all around.
The sounds of joy cannot be forever lost, they will be found.

When we miss a loved one that has passed on to glory,
We can always listen for some music from their familiar story.
Hear about their adventures and successes by the score.
All we need do is to open up memory's door.

We will, in time, let our tears wash away the gloom.
And then for those joyous memories there will be more room.
That special laugh and that crooked grin...
Actually, the line of our separation is very thin.

It's just over the rainbow and up Jacob's ladder.
Go there whenever you can... Anytime, it doesn't matter.
The angels are in charge of memories; they handle them with care.
They know with the value of a memory, nothing can compare.

Someday, my friend, when we both have the time,
I'd like to share one of my memories that, of course,
Is in a rhyme.

Cheer

As a little girl, my mom made a gift for me.
It was a bracelet of buttons finally set free.
No longer on a Sunday school dress that I outgrew
Or my old pj's with the bear buttons...his name was Boo-Boo.
There was a button from my tap shoes of childhood days.
This is a reminder that you can't have talent in all ways.

Little buttons that bring lovely memories...thought after thought.
None of which can ever be purchased or bought.
They develop overtime with patience and love,
And are held safe in our heart by the Father above
Now when I need a lift...a bit of joy in my life,
I have a small reminder that there is an end to strife.

I take my childhood bracelet...now showing some age,
And I review every button like a book with a page
I go back many years...where did all that time go?
Everyone needs a bracelet so their memories can flow.
It's a reminder of the past that holds moments so dear.
It will summon up in you pure, instant cheer.

Maybe just say a prayer and ask the Father to help you.
When we are happy, I'm sure he is, too!

Music to Your Ear

The dog's excited bark when you return home at the end of day,
He's all ready for a walk and wants a time for play.

The hoot of an owl in the depth of a dark night,
As he stops to rest from his long nocturnal flight.

Thunder as it grumbles and lightening crack,
And pounding rain as it pours down without any slack.

Music to your ear.

A baby's cry for attention and care...
What a beautiful sound that we can share.

The door opening with the old squeak we expect to hear,
Telling us that a loved one is home now, safe and near.

When all the house is quiet with everyone going to sleep,
Now you can say your "My soul to keep."

Music to your ear.

Organ music so beautiful your heart will lurch,
As you quietly sit in the very house of God, your own church.

Listen, the birds are putting music in our surrounding air,
Giving us a concert we can hear from our own lawn chair.

The event of a new life...be it a boy or a girl,
Will turn all of your life into a musical whirl!

Music to your ear.

Just the very voice of my spouse after many a year,
When he says "I love you" is music to prompt a tear.

That sound when I awake at the first morning light
When the earth is stretching and the sun is reaching new
    height.

Nature has a voice so loud and ever so clear,
With many sounds that we should hold dear.

Music to your ear.

Have you listened to children as they talk to each other?
Seems they consider all around them to be a brother.

Often it will be a simple sound that touches your very soul,
Maybe it could even redirect your life's stroll.

I've mentioned just a few of the beautiful sounds you can hear.
Why not add them to your life? It could surely be...

Music to your ear.

A Feather

Life is so fragile, like a feather in flight,
Floating on the breeze in the bright sunlight.

Going this way and that...gliding along,
Sometimes weak and other times strong.

Twisting and turning in its swirling trip,
Dancing and diving with an occasional dip.

Once in a while it might stop to hover,
While being kissed by snow as a newfound lover.

Alas, its flight will end as it joins the ground,
Doing this gently without a sound.

Now to rejoin the earth's cycle of life.
Its next journey, however, will be free from strife.

Eternal Mentor

Abba travels with me all of the time,
And often there with an impossible rhyme.
Occasionally testing my "Send me. Send me."
In his loving way, saying, "We'll see…we'll see."

He is the spark that lights a thought
And the long lost memory recalling what I was once taught.
He's the balm of forgiveness, soothing and warm,
The extended arm to hold me from harm.

He's the quiet time I need to visit with my soul,
Helping me with his patience to see my goal.
Without him I am a mere empty shell,
Not a place at all for worthy thoughts to dwell.

But then when our hands join and the walk begins,
The directions we take are far away from greed, hate, and
    sins.
When I have a weak moment, I feel him near.
When I'm afraid, he helps me with my fear.

He is my friend, my savior, the keeper of my soul.
My mentor for all eternity is his role.

An Old Rag Doll

I wonder, did God make the flower for the bee
Or the other way around? Let me see.
Certainly, when the Lord created all of his flowers,
It just had to be some of his finest hours.
The beauty, the colors, the delicate form,
And certainly with its fragrance, your heart will warm.

But then, on the other hand, what about the bee?
Honey from the flowers is his food, seems to me.
All the Lord's decisions and choices are really so deep,
Wonder if he still has time each night "My soul to keep."
But then he's my Abba, my shepherd, my eternal friend.
I don't have a problem that he can't mend.

I'm like an old rag doll repaired time after time.
On the open market, surely, I'm not worth a thin dime.
But he came to save even the least of these.
To all men, he offers his miraculous ease.
When in trouble, God will help you endure.
He loves each and every old rag doll, that's for sure.

Books

Books serve a multitude of purposes in this life,
Recording our history and reviewing all our strife.
Giving directions and descriptions to places worldwide
Or giving our phone number and address so we can't hide.

Presenting fiction at its very wildest and best,
And how every superhero is able to stand the test.
Hard covers or paperbacks...whatever be the style,
May they hold our interest for a very long while.

Some large size books can have values not worth a cent,
While a small book often holds a huge content.
Mountains of text books surround us twenty-four-seven.
So many that they could possibly serve as steps to heaven.

Books are helpers we use to cook or to build a house
Or help us invent a better trap to catch a mouse.
Grandma said to read some books with a grain of salt.
When paving life's road, always use the best asphalt!

Now there is one book you can trust for sure.
It's been around for thousands of years...it will endure.
The words came from the Master of all the earth.
He is its Creator and gave it it's worth.

He even died for it, the story is in his book.
Now what could it hurt for you to take a little look?
It has many directions on how we should live.
And tells you all about how to share and give.

It has been on the best seller list for years and years,
And has helped those lost and dried many tears.
I guess, by now, you know it's the Bible of which I speak.
Why not get it down from the shelf and take a peek?

After all, what can it harm to just take a look?
I think you'll find a very special story in this book.

Today

Some days start out easy...others not so much.
This a.m. has begun with what I'd call a frantic touch.
Someone is feeling not at all very well,
When the day begins with moaning, you can always tell.

That's when you switch gears to another speed.
Suddenly your attention is drawn to those in need.
A pill, an ice bag, or maybe just a kind word,
Or a very sad story that needs to be heard.

Whatever the problem, you can handle it for sure.
Every situation always has a definite cure.
What a great way to start this fantastic day.
Maybe I'll pray first and see what God has to say.

Together we can handle this next twenty-four
Because our Father has the key to every possible door.
May this annual holiday bring you every blessing,
Including a large plate of turkey and dressing!

PS: Today, this calendar date is marked Thanksgiving.
What an interesting life we are surely living.

Love

My words are in a bit of a battle today.
Seems they don't fit together in the same way.
Their meanings haven't changed in Mr. Webster's book,
But somehow now they have an evolving outlook.
I guess you could say they've had a change in attitude.
Some are now haughty...they've reached a new latitude.

Strange how that happens over many, many years,
As words survive fear and trauma, joy, and tears.
But I humbly believe some of them should stay the same.
I'm thinking of the small word of love by name.
However, could the meaning of love undergo a change,
All those sweet, precious feelings undergo a rearrange?

Your love can no longer be completely whole, your all?
In the list of emotions, love will no longer stand as tall?
Will it no longer play a starring role in our life?
How else will I get through all my earthly strife?
Aren't we the ones who make love important, anyway?
About its status surely we should have something to say!

Then there is God with his eternal love to treasure.
Now that surely has no ruler long enough to measure.
I've decided love's meaning will survive all the ages.
It will write its beautiful history over all life's pages.
We, the children of a heavenly Father from above,
Will always hold precious the word of love.

A Jar to Fill

As we approach God's heavenly throne,
We will each carry a jar or bottle all our own.
In it will be who we were...every gift and strife.
A captured witness to how well we lived our life.

Our final choice will be the words we write on our jar.
In a simple word or two, we can describe who and what we are.
Like a granny with her mason jar just reading "humbled"
Or a boy with his firefly jar having a crack labeled, "sorry
    stumbled".

My container is unimportant as I can see,
So long as my jar holds a pen and words, send me.
Think of the multitude of vessels of all size and odd shape,
Some even damaged and showing a bit of tape.

I like to think God lines them all up on his own pantry shelf
And reviews them in a quiet time all by himself.
My dear husband confessed his jar would simply say, thank you.
And that would describe his working life...every nut, bolt, and
    screw.

I hope you didn't forget something that should be in your jar
Because, my friend, there is no going back...the journey is too far.
So just join the crowd and wait your turn,
There could be a few things you have yet to learn.

Let's hope it's not too late and your chance has passed.
Before you know it, life can be gone so fast.
Well, it's time I get to work. I've a jar to fill, you know.
Our heavenly Father is always busy and keeps me on the go.

Rearrange

I wrote Help on the steamy bathroom mirror today.
I had such a tough problem...what can I say?
Then I went about my life and realized my problem wasn't very
   tall.
In fact, right now, I would call it somewhat small.

I'm sure in this story you find no heavenly hand,
But to you, dear friend, I say, aren't miracles grand?
They usually aren't like a train ripping through a crowd,
But miracles are quiet, sweet moments, many are not even out
   loud.

You haven't witnessed any of these in your life?
Perhaps you are just concentrating on your strife.
Sometimes we must lift our head up out of the sinful sand
And listen to God conducting his heavenly band.

There are birds singing, children playing, and wind through the
   trees.
His music is everywhere for you... I'll just mention these.
Once you start looking around, your steamy mirror won't seem
   strange.
It's God giving your life a little rearrange.

The Drum

Bobby had a little drum...blue and red.
He would beat it fiercely and march around his bed.
Said he wanted to be a soldier someday
And go to places that were far, far away.
As time passed, the little drum was set aside.
And later still, Bob was an eagle scout with pride.

College, cars, and his first love,
He was surely a son sent from above.
But soon the ugly word war entered his life.
He saw the death and destruction in its strife.
Then Bob answered that noble call to arms,
To conquer the evil that always harms.

Now in a uniform, for his country he stood,
Ready to defend...he would do what he could.
Saying "goodbye" to his loved ones here,
He asked God to help him with his fear.
A thousand miles away Bob sees war...
The pain and loss and the slow-healing scar.

Our prayers are with him and all the others.
They are our fathers, mothers, kids, and brothers.
They carry Old Glory into the battles' fray,
So all the world might share a peaceful day.
Little Bob came back but had lost a limb.
However, his patriotism did not dim.

So should you see him along your way,
Why not say, "Hey…you have a good day.
Thanks for helping protect this great land.
I'd sure be proud to shake your hand."
Bob is an American, whatever might come,
And he's still that little boy beating his drum.

Seeds

Sometimes when an old seed is all tuckered out,
Dry and withered and passed it's time, you have no doubt.
Grandma would say, "It just needs water it feels used up.
A little drink will make it perky as a brand-new pup!"

We know all growing begins in that special part—
Our gift from the Father we call our heart.
Once in a while we need to visit this outstanding place,
To put a smile on our heart's face.

Changing your mind...every woman knows,
That we do it every time the wind blows!
Man's best growing is always done deep inside.
That's where his soul and conscience do abide.

When we offer a sip of kindness to an unhappy friend,
We help his sadness to find an end.
Always remember about a seed's finest hour.
That's the very moment it turns into a beautiful flower.

Play Pretend

I heard my soul singing today,
As I watched a little child at play.
She was swaying in the old porch swing,
And suddenly became the queen of everything.
Her baby was crying; although no one hears.
That's because dolls only shed pretend tears.
The swing was her carriage...make believe is never wrong.
I couldn't tell her I was a little too old to belong.
Somewhere in life I almost lost my pretend mode.
I often wondered if that loss ever showed.
Time was I could travel far, far away
And life would become whatever I'd say...
A castle, white and shiny, atop a beautiful hill,
With pretty birds perched on each window sill
And every room with a dog of my choice.
I could sing to them with a pretend voice.
They did tricks, and when it was time for a nap,
I would sleep with two or three on my lap.
I had a giant ice cream cone for lunch
And the dogs had biscuits on which to munch.
Flowers there were bigger and smelled the best.
I picked large bouquets as I pursued my quest.
The bees buzzed around but wouldn't sting...
The whole big world was my plaything.

Then came time I'd hear mom's voice... I knew,
This day's adventure was now through.
So now when life around me gets tough,
When my mood tells me I've had enough,
I make a secret journey back to that childhood place,
With its simple childish joy that does much to erase
All the woes and grief grown-up life can give.
And, yes, I shall go back there so long as I live.

PS: Dipped into childhood
Memories!

Do-Re-Mi

Beautiful notes, please, surround me...cover my being.
Today I wish for no sadness to obstruct my seeing.
Let me float on your lilting sound...
And see your brilliant colors all around.

Each note of your melodic scale colored bright and rich
And all sharps and flats placed in an appropriate niche.
May your notes join to form friendly chords
That will bring a new life to old keyboards.

Let the music travel inside me to a deeply buried place
Where I put only good memories and a happy face.
Soon I'll start to relive thoughts from the past,
And then pray that this moment could last and last.

I listen for little grace notes, so quick and sweet,
While my foot is constantly keeping the beat.
I'm lifted from this earth to swing and sway...
Music has its magic way of changing work to play.

I'll listen carefully to each distinctive note.
In this musical election, each has its own vote.
Each will show its colors, then take its place
On the musical scores' well-written face.

Red, blue, yellow, orange, and green...
As he created, these are the colors God must have seen.
Notes were assigned to a color to blend and explore
And show us the way to a rainbow's heavenly door.

Those deep, low notes, reassuring and always strong,
Are trying to tell us that all of life isn't wrong.
There are dark moments in just a few measures,
But mostly the music is filled with colorful treasures.

Music has powers to bring a big smile
And many tunes stay with you for a very long while.
There are those notes that cause you to drop a tear
And hymns that tell you that your God is always near.

A patriotic march brings forward your national pride.
Music has a language all its own and it's worldwide.
So A through G God knew that's how his music would be...
Pure beauty to hear and a stunning rainbow to see.

Music is everywhere and with color it abounds.
This gift for man is never far away...just listen for the sounds.
My friend, I wish you rainbows and music every day.
Our heavenly Father created it just that way.

PS: As a child I learned to sing it as Do-Re-Mi.
Then, of course, I might have been just a bit off key!

Just Be There

Most times I think, Just be there.
Simply sit with me...just pull up a chair.

No fancy gifts, your smile will do,
As long as that silly grin belongs to you.

We don't have to travel from this place.
Anywhere is fine, so long as I see your face.

Words hardly seem to count
When with one touch emotions meant.

I know you're coming by the sound of your walk,
And body language is much better than talk.

When I'm lost in thought, you somehow know,
Ready to share...quietly waiting in my shadow.

I'm sure these gifts came from all our years together...
Many joys and a few tears we had to weather.

I shan't ask for more…not from this earth.
God has blessed us with all things of worth.

Our love is a gift we will always share…
So long as I know you'll just be there.

PS: Only I am blessed to know the miracle of this poem.

It Only Takes One

It takes but one mind to change many,
So every million must start with a penny.
Between that one and the multitude, there is strength
To run the distance and finish the length.
That special gift of inner strength and power
Is surely a person's golden hour.
When he sees the right and walks straight ahead.
Remember, few men lead...most are led.
It's with purpose and heart that a job is done,
Then dread is dispelled by a shining sun.

Be the one who leads, always true to self,
Never unconcerned, and resting on the shelf.
Wars were won...victories were made
By those who went forward, dedicated and unafraid.
My source of strength comes from above
Because I'm sure of God's eternal love.
I cannot always be in the lead,
But I'll be there to help whatever the need.
So, at the end of a most trying day,
I'll be proud I acted in a positive way.

Little Rhymes

My poems are at the very root of me.
Coming forward from deep inside, I set them free.
Often, they flower with joy and gladness,
Sometimes displaying a moment of my madness.
At these times, all objects can speak out loud,
And there's a moving figure in each single cloud.
I reach back in memory to the years of my youth.
The times I got money for pulling a loose tooth.

That's when an ice cream cone was a five-cent treat,
And jumping Double Dutch was quite a feat.
Waking up in the morning to the rattle of dishes
And blowing out candles making birthday wishes.
I remember flying a kite in the big open field,
Getting red in the sun and my nose all peeled.
Sand stores, story hours, and monopoly games,
And your friends calling you silly, made-up names.

And then there were paper dolls... I had Betty Grable.
I'd line up all my sets on the dining room table
And dress and redress them to suit myself.
When I tired of them, they went back on the shelf.
I remember my bicycle...it was blue and white.
Going fast down the hills, I was quite a sight.
Bubble baths, hot dogs, and Mom's cherry pie...

Now those are things for which a kid would die.
We were easily satisfied in those childhood years
When parents were there to wipe away our tears,
To solve the problems or do a quick mend,
I guess then we thought that would never end.
But growing up comes quickly…with few delays.
And responsibility replaces our carefree days.
It's good sometimes to recall past times.
I guess that's why I write these little rhymes.

The Matchbox

It was a little matchbox hanging on the wall,
Not up very high because she wasn't tall.
Every morning she'd strike a match on its' side
To make a fire for the bacon she always fried.
She also lit the kerosene lamp on the table,
So at early morn she would see, as well as able.

These actions began her busy pioneer day,
Whether skies were sunny or they looked gray.
She still marveled at that tiny invention,
Giving fire a brand-new extension.
Transported easily in her apron pocket,
Almost as easy as she wore her mother's locket.

This new land made it difficult to live.
Often taking more from a man than he could give.
But for today she had her list of things to get done
That would keep her busy till the setting sun.
First, make a bonfire for wash water to heat,
For soon her husband would bring home some meat.

She often wondered about that little match...
A burst of flame from one little scratch.
What was this world coming to...growing so fast,
Stretching out over territory so rich and vast?
The talk of gold and trappers galore,
Would they someday even need to lock their door?

Man was created with talents, not tapped.
Challenges and inventions not yet unwrapped.
God gives us changes in little pieces and bits...
As much as our space in time permits.
As she looked at her matchbox on the wall,
She was with her family...with them all.

The matchbox was a gift from her mother.
She would keep it forever...there could be no other.
They were on an adventure heading to the sea,
Her husband at her side and a child to be.
Necessity, the mother of invention...you bet,
And with God's help, the need is always met.

So should you see a small matchbox...recall its' worth.
It served an important purpose upon this earth.

Home

Help is always waiting there,
Our family is ready to help and share.
Maybe you've made a big mistake...
Even so, we love you for your sake.

So smile and move along life's way,
With joy in your heart day after day.
Every problem has an answer somewhere,
Even if we don't see it, it's still there.
Time has a way of helping our strife.

Home gives us a reason to live our life.
Owing to no one but giving when needed,
Meeting our problems...never defeated.
Enter that door...no need to roam
     Because now, my friend, you have come home.

The Dress

I had a new dress for Christmas night.
It was plaid and looked like the colors were having a fight.
But Mom liked it...said it went with my hair.
For flaming red tresses, it was what I should wear.

The shoes were another story, indeed.
So tight I truly thought my feet would bleed.
I managed to avoid a large hair ribbon of sort.
It couldn't help the fact that I was so short.

That night I had a speech to say in church,
And nothing should my efforts faintly besmirch.
Frightened beyond any human reality
And feeling as though I might be a Christmas fatality.

I somehow rose to the occasion, as one would say,
And started my recitation come what may.
When it was over and we finally went home,
I had a moment to carry forever...where'er I roam.

Memories are often like that...made with some pain.
But I believe those are the ones that really remain.
That dress I wore has long passed away.
But I shall never forget that Christmas day.

I still see my parents sitting there so proud.
Surely the most nervous people in the whole crowd.
I knew I was doing it just for those two.
They were only there to see me through.

Isn't it great...the memories we keep?
Those wonderful occasions that run so deep.
Defying the passage of time and space,
They take us back to a special place.

This was such a sweet moment, I must confess,
And it started with tight shoes and a plaid Christmas dress.

PS: Immanuel memories,
sixth grade
Mr. Herpolshimer's class

Dogs

What a noble beast God made that day.
Surely, he used some special kind of clay.
With big kind eyes and ever-wagging tail,
Always there to greet us without fail.
Gifted with just a bark and a seldom-heard howl,
And wearing a face that can't form a scowl.

His affection at your fingertips...you just pet
And you'll receive a sloppy kiss, I bet!
He knows when you're sad and will sit with you.
He'll wear a sad look just like you do.
He touches our heart in a peaceful way,
There are no words he need ever say.

He asks for so little yet offers so much,
And gives our heart a special touch.
He will stay and sit, beg and fetch,
And just throw a ball...he's there to catch!
He's at your side when the world dumps on you
Because dogs have this invisible magical glue.

It holds them firmly in your heart,
And of your life he's an important part.
Giving his all...asking little in return,
A companion at your side at every turn.
When God made the dog, he had no regrets,
Knowing he'd be a champion among all pets.

So when his days finally see an end,
He'll go to heaven and wait for his friend.

A Floppy Gray Rabbit

He was a floppy gray rabbit that used to be blue
And was stored in a box with an old baby shoe.
He had faded with time...his stuffing falling out.
So old he'd forgotten what Easter was all about.

Spending dark years in a closet tucked away
And giving up on ever having a brighter day.
Suddenly resurrected and brought into the light,
This new career gave him quite a bit of fright.

His faded color was perked up with a bright pink bow
And he was set in a big basket so he would show.
On green paper grass with eggs all around,
A mix of confusion and joy in him did abound.

Surely no one wanted him...he was truly worn out,
And everything new and pretty is what Easter is about.
Our little rabbit found a special spot that day
In a different home some distance away.

He was placed in the hands of a person with age,
Almost like being set on a huge center stage.
The face was wrinkled but the eyes he knew...
Younger eyes he remembered from when he was still blue.

A little boy...this was that small boy of long ago.
His eyes still had that mischievous glow.
Well, what do you know? We're back together,
Both of us look like we've seen a lot of weather.

I won't see his wrinkles if he doesn't notice my fade,
But neither of us is fit for any Easter parade.
Still we have sweet memories that we can both share...
Me in my basket and he in his chair.

Down through the years, they go back there again.
It's that story that begins with "Remember when."

Choices

Wow, I actually won the lottery today,
But not the money kind, I guess, I should say.

I just looked around me...a lot I've failed to see.
And best of all, these gifts are free.

So many silver stars and bunches of golden flowers,
Enough to keep me happy for hours and hours.

I guess I got busy and passed them by,
These wonderful things money can't buy.

Bunnies and butterflies, bees and birds,
Their beauty is more than I can describe in words.

And all those grins and smiles directed my way,
That will always help to save a disappointing day.

I could help, too...spreading joy like a soft spring rain.
And if everyone did, this would form a chain.

It would wrap around this world, brave and strong,
And lessen the effect of all things that are wrong.

I'm not too sure money can do just that.
It can't replace a kiss and a little love pat.

So...if given a choice between God's creations or lots of money,
I might just choose a soft, white Easter bunny.

PS: A little foolish, I guess,
But... Happy Easter
2012

On with the Show

The sun breaks through the still sleeping sky,
And tells the birds, "Get up. It's time to fly."
Flowers raise their heads and start to bloom.
For more of their delicate beauty, God always makes room.

This time is called morning...the start of another day.
I know most of us wish that it could all be play.
But as the day progresses, our talents roll out.
That's how we're made...what life is all about.

What you can't do...someone else will be able.
There is a variety of food choices on a well set table.
When we all work together, so much can be done,
So much joy can be shared by the next setting sun.

Surely, you want to be a part of this great twenty-four.
There's a special skill you can bring to the floor.
Presented well today, you will grow and learn.
But don't worry...you'll know when it's your turn.

Sometimes it's scary and we don't want to budge,
But God gives us that tiny heavenly nudge.
And suddenly there you are right in the front row,
And God is saying, "On with the show!"

Life's Thread

Take the label off of your hope.
Whatever life's outcome you can cope.
Just the act of looking ahead is a good start,
And that's where hope plays a major part.

Faith in action sets the wheels of hope going,
Gets all those survival juices flowing.
Alone? Don't be silly...we are never alone.
We are made of tough fabric and very well sewn.

Our tailor did his finest work on all of us.
Yet often we walk in circles and continue to fuss.
Why not just have faith and he'll redirect your confusion,
Help us find that path that leads to a conclusion.

It might not be just what you had in mind,
But his answers are best...let it up to him to find.
Put your faith and hope in Jesus. He'll lead you ahead.
Remember, your Creator has a firm grip on your life's thread.

Dreaming

When sleep alludes, I escape to a cloud...
Floating soft and white, a creation to make God proud.
I snuggle down into it and have sweet dreams
Where all is calm in the sky's shining night beams.

A little twinkling star serves as my night light,
And my mind turns away from all hate and fight.
The full moon is my window to the entire universe.
Only then with every living creature I converse.

I fall asleep on a celestial pillow, hearing an angel's lullaby
While rocked in the great cradle called the sky.
I won't need a pill or potion to find blessed sleep.
I just retire into my soul...quiet and deep.

My father always keeps my soul until the morning hour.
It's then my eyes open like a new budding flower.
During the night hours I'm nurtured by heaven above.
As I sleep, I'm covered with God's blanket of love.

All the while a soft, warm breeze drifts quietly by,
Stirred by angel wings as they fly.
In this place of miracles I find perfect peace.
It's here that eternal joy will never, ever cease.

Now, yes, a dream, but someday I think not.
Up there, somewhere, God has reserved for me a spot.
It's then, every night I shall sleep on a cloud
Because he will take his children home as long ago he vowed.

Friends

Friends laughing together...a wonderful sound
When joy and love truly do abound.

When the sun seems brighter and heaven nearer,
Faithful friends, what could possibly be dearer?

Time spent together are moments you'll always treasure.
Friendship was God's creation to give happiness without measure.

When a sadness comes, friends are there to share,
Help to make the bad times easier to bear.

Just a simple smile, a word, a touch...
This coming from a friend means so very much.

Friends are the gift that God gives us every day.
Call them buddy or pal...just wonderful is what I'd say.

Well, I'll draw this little poem to an end...
I might just go out shopping with a friend.

Honey and Oggie

Made by Grandma many years ago,
They were constant companions to a boy named Joe.
They went on trips and in the sandbox, too,
And suffered through pottie training when Joe was two.
Always there when tears were being shed,
And every night they shared his bed.
They've been dropped and walked upon,
Now and again just drug along.

Even in the hospital they took that first shot
To prove to Joey it didn't really hurt a lot.
They shared his lap at his story hour,
And once were forgotten in a warm spring shower.
That's what toys do...they form a bond
That goes through childhood and even beyond.
Never any complaining that could be heard,
These two friends endured without a word.

It was Honey and Oggie, always there to save.
Sometimes this Bunny and Doggie got less than they gave.
But they were hugged till totally threadbare,
And loved every minute...they were there to share.
Honey's one ear was a bit ragged, you know,
From Joey's teething days but it didn't show.
They served as pillows every once in a while,
And were even rescued from a dark theater aisle.

As the years passed, eyes, nose, and hair were lost,
But both brave toys stayed with Joe at any cost.
They recalled being placed in a big backpack
For a short trip...then coming right back.
It was Joe's driver's test...an important feat,
And he wanted Honey and Oggie in the back seat.
Now those times are gone and Joey's left home.
They can't imagine where on this earth he will roam.

They're retired now...but truly miss that little boy.
They are sure, however, the best life is that of a toy!
Burped and peed on, hugged and kissed...
It was a great life they wouldn't have missed.
So next time you see a toy that's all worn out,
You'll know where it's been and what it's all about.
Maybe, could you just sit them up on a shelf,
Where they can have a rest and be proud of themself?

Better still...do you have a Honey or Oggie somewhere?
Why not get them out so they can share?

Faith and Hope

Lord, when I asked for a miracle, you gave me hope.
Like skiing, it's best to start on the bunny slope.

Then little by little I see the best way ahead.
We never get the butter before the bread.

Noah asked for a fleet, he got just one big boat
Because God knew that faith and hope would keep him afloat.

These two always will work well together.
Then we'll get through the worst kind of weather.

David had faith in his God and hope in that stone.
With such a combination, no one stands alone.

Look around for your faith, it's still there...
In the corner of your heart, with hope, they like to share.

Well, I enjoyed the chat...hold tight to your faith and hope.
And we could meet again...maybe on the bunny slope.

Tags

There was Benjamin Bear with a tag on his tail,
Sitting on a table at a big garage sale.
He had never been the favorite, he was sure of that.
While all the others played, he usually just sat.
Maybe it was his size...he was quite small.
Surely not like the giraffe who was so tall.
But he was kinda cute, he had heard it said...
Seems this was only good for sitting on a bed.

But today was the day he'd say goodbye.
He was kind of sad and thought he might cry.
Where would he go? Who would want him?
Tiny tears filled his eyes to their very brim.
His tag said a quarter...that wasn't very much.
And at that moment he felt a soft touch.
A hand picked him up, turning him all around.
He held his little breath, not making a sound.

It was an older lady...her hair was quite gray.
She didn't look like she would even like to play.
But she paid the money and he went in a bag.
He guessed the 25¢ was alright on his tag.
Her house was something, let me tell you.
She had a lot of bears...maybe a hundred or two.
I got to sit in the lap of this much bigger bear
Who had a coat of plush expensive kind of hair.

He said the button in his ear was a pedigree.
Only the tag on my tail identified me!
He was a fancy, sought-after bear.
But we did agree that all of life was not fair.
Outsides don't count, I found that out.
Having a good heart is what it's all about.
I'm proud of my tag that says twenty-five cents.
Anyway, money will never give you real confidence.

Now day in and out Ben sits with Joe,
And you can just watch their friendship grow,
With the little bear learning from the other.
Despite a tag or buttons, he was a brother.
They taught each other about values and such
And that really money didn't mean that much.
Ben costs a quarter... Joe, a lot more,
But when you're friends, who keeps score?

PS: Found Ben at a garage sale; knew his name the minute
I saw him. The young man who sold him was named Ben,
also—who knows? Ben and Joe now reside side by side in an
upstairs bedroom. I feel I caught their spirit in this poem.
Hope you enjoy it!

Heavenly Crutches

Today I would like to walk with a little child.
What do we often call them...meek and mild?
But they still have qualities that we long ago lost,
Once the road from child to adult has been crossed.

The innocence is gone and we find defiance in its place,
And we begin to see guilt written on another's face.
We become more cautious...now we first ask why.
No more a child with his kite flying happily in the sky.

Remember how that felt to be so free,
To really know the person you call me?
To say "Excuse me" the way your mother said,
And don't forget the prayers when you went to bed.

Always share...it's the right thing to do.
Sometimes I didn't want to...how about you?
And manners aren't for sissies, but they're no fun.
I feel like I might be the only one!

I should give up my chair for a grown-up to sit
When I can see by his size he's not going to fit!
Mom says when a hanky is hard for me to retrieve,
I should never go on and use my sleeve.

Well, what are sleeves for? They seem kinda handy,
And I can tell you they really work dandy!
I guess being a kid is fun...gotta always wait your turn.
I'll be all grown-up before I finally learn!

I'll think a little more about those bedtime prayers.
This Jesus seems like a friend that really cares.
Maybe he'll help me with my manners and such.
Sometimes a kid just needs a heavenly crutch.

PS: The child came forward today
And had just a little bit to say.
(GIG) (GOD IS GOOD)

Aren't Prayers Great?

One size prayer usually fits all
And every one of them will help you feel tall.
Aren't prayers great?

I'm talking about having your strength renewed
And your confidence in life reviewed.
Aren't prayers great?

A brief one might even replace a tear
And give you some time of sweet cheer.
Aren't prayers great?

Just a little talk can give you joyous hope
And you see a way that will help you cope.
Aren't prayers great?

When your hurt goes so very deep
And you have trouble with your sleep.
Aren't prayers great?

When fear seizes you in its' grip,
What a joy to take this quiet trip.
Aren't prayers great?

Often we just simply lose our way.
Everywhere we turn the future seems so gray.
Aren't prayers great?

His grace lights a new pathway to walk.
Just hold his hand and begin to talk.
Aren't prayers great?

Prayers give us the time to stop and think
When we believe we're at the lowest we can sink.
Aren't prayers great?

When we must be brave and just keep going
With the heavy burden that we are towing.
Aren't prayers great?

When you stand alone, oh, I've been there.
You just reach out for Jesus to share.
Aren't prayers great?

I've taken one of his prayers and changed it a bit
And use it quite often as I quietly sit...

"The Lord is my shepherd, I shall not want.
He makes me sit down at my kitchen table,
He leads me to a pen and paper,
He restores my soul."
                    Amen!

Aren't prayers great?

Slip and Fall

Ever slip and fall down in the snow
And got up quick so no one would know?
You brush yourself off and resume your travel.
Funny how a little slip can cause your day to unravel.

Maybe the only thing that hurts is just your pride.
Sometimes that's a thing very hard to hide.
The slip could be a cruel word said to a friend.
Often those errors are hard to mend.

And then there's the time you told that little lie,
Then felt so ashamed you just wanted to cry.
A slip of the tongue happens so very fast,
But it's effects travel on to last and last.

Putting mind before mouth might be a good thought.
You think that, especially when you get caught.
Well, my friend, you have an extraordinary day.
Just don't slip and fall...watch what you say!

PS: Don't forget, should you happen to slip and fall,
Sending a little prayer could help to fix it all.

Love Is...

Love is so strong...like a lion in rage,
And wise as an ancient, all-knowing sage.
Love is patient, and will wait forever,
And stay by your side, leave you never.

God's love stands tall with endless height.
It's the miracle that gives little birds their first flight.
Love can just be a smile that warms your heart,
But of your day, could be the very best part.

Love is so gentle it could mend butterfly wings,
And with the touch of its hand, your very soul sings.
Often love is just a look...a glance with no word said.
That alone softens away a day full of dread.

Sweet puppies will kiss you right on your face.
That's love, too, but comes from a different place.
Love is a birth, a wedding, or a final goodbye.
God is in everything under his blue sky.

Love is a colorful flower smiling up at you,
And also when you help a small child tie his shoe.
Love kisses boo-boos and wipes away many tears
And chases away the bogeyman and all the fears.

Love is contagious... why not pass it around?
It's one of the dearest feelings ever to be found.
Love hopes and helps and always prays.
It's a constant running through all of your days.

I'm hoping a little love comes to you from my pen.
I try to pass it on that way, now and again.
Maybe when your heart is full of love and can swell no more,
You might find yourself standing at heaven's door.

What a perfectly beautiful place for us to be.
Just think about who we are about to see.
Here we can experience pure love with no hesitation.
Aren't we glad we made our reservation?

The Best Parts

It's going to be a joyous beautiful day
Because all of God's music is ready to play.
Every sound, every beat has a perfect place,
Blessed and sent ahead on the wings of his grace.

Wind through the trees offers a cool humming sound.
And all nature sings, even small insects underground.
The concert is beginning at the sun's direction
And the music is perfect...of course, it's God's selection.

Sea waves roaring and birds calling their mate
And the hooting owls are having a debate.
Some are quiet sounds...listen. Don't pass them by.
You could hear the fluttering wings of a monarch butterfly.

Hear the buzz of a tiny bee with its head in a flower,
And what's better than hearing the warm drops of a spring shower?
Once in a while, you may get to hear a baby's first cry...
That's a sound to bring a tear to any eye.

Then there's the roar of thunder and lightning's crack
Or the chirp of a thousand crickets on a night so black.
God gave us each two ears...let's use them well.
What sounds he sends you, who can tell?

We should always listen with loving hearts,
Then we can be sure to hear the very best parts.

Fourscore

I'm so old now, I count my years by the score.
If you're interested, I'm already up to four.
Did I live it well? That's hard to say.
I usually worked and played on the appropriate day
And gave the Lord his praise to start my week.
Can't say, though, I was always among the meek.

I voiced my opinions when an audience was there.
A valuable point seems important to share.
There were times my mustard seed got oh so lost.
And on the world's sea of misery, I was tossed.
"Live and learn," that's what the old-timers said,
And I didn't always like the way I made my bed.

I've met many people as I travelled through my years,
Held a lot of hands and wiped a few tears.
Said a kind word when the moment seemed right
And tried to avoid any silly little fight.
Well, now that I'm here, Lord...am I truly wise?
I've gotten old... I thought wisdom was the prize!

You mean it can miss a generation along the way?
Well, I better check my life's map without delay.
Maybe I missed a few turns...got in a hurry.
Sometimes my motives did seem a bit blurry.
I'll retrace my steps, open a new door,
And try to stay around for another score!

Standing Tall

Today this old head seems in such a swirl,
So many thoughts are all in a whirl.
Time to part them and find each a place,
See which is the first one that I must now face.

The moment is at hand and it waits for no man.
You know, this was part of God's overall plan.
We're presented a problem and given some time,
And he watches us as up the hills we climb.

Often we are clumsy and slip and sometimes fall.
But just keep trying...if you can't walk, then crawl.
Experience teaches difficult lessons that we are to learn,
And no matter our life's station, we have a turn.

I wonder, have we learned something from events past?
It might be well for those memories to last.
They could serve us well if we happen to have trouble.
Life isn't perfect...or did I burst your bubble?

But we can learn from the tough experience part,
And then gently tuck the sweet stuff into our heart.
Then when things turn bad, just go to your heart and rest
And get ready for yet another worldly test.

To solve our problems, there are a number of ways.
But we will need the time God gives...those precious days.
So maybe we should pray for a long, long life.
How else could we handle all the strife?

We will never live long enough to learn it all...
But then our God is the only one who really stands tall.

Color My World

I watched a great-granddaughter coloring in her book.
If only I could have bottled up that extraordinary look.
It was one of joy coupled with interest and care.
At this moment, she had a project...she could not share.
The sky must be a special joining of several blues.
And the rainbow, her own creation of colorful hues.

Only in that book could the world be as she desires...
A kaleidoscope of colors that never tires,
That changes with her mood and expresses her feelings,
And is never bothered with troublesome dealings.
Far too soon, she'll grow up and sadly close those pages.
In life, she'll now be on much bigger stages.

All of the colors will not be of her selection.
Her pathway will often turn its direction.
Some of the colors may not always be her choice,
But she will find a way to put a rainbow in her voice.
As she grows, all shades will become that much clearer.
Oh, yes, and hopefully they will be all the dearer.

May she walk amidst the beautiful colors in her life
And find relief in them from this world's strife.
The red of a rose, a silver star, the blue bird with his song.
All of God's colors are so perfect...none are wrong.
It was his special gift to man at the creation...
To give us colors for the earth's duration.

So each time your sky is black and you've lost the way,
Just ask God to color my world...that's all you need to say.

Jesus Did It

Miracles are here around us every day,
They help us to live our life, work, or play.
And just like one sibling tells on the other...
Putting the blame on a sister or little brother.
So I must tell the truth and admit,
All these flowers and beautiful trees... Jesus did it!

You know that warm sun that greets us at dawn,
Just as we get up and have that final yawn...
Jesus did it!

And what about those stars twinkling in the sky?
Look hard enough and you'll find a moon nearby...
Jesus did it!

Warm sweet rain showers in the early spring
And colorful birds that chirp and sing...
Jesus did it!

That chubby little child struggling to tie his shoe,
Wonder who put that sweet scene in front of you?
Jesus did it!

You somehow find the right words to comfort a friend.
Our Father has answers to problems without end.
Jesus did it!

When I pray on my knees and feel his grace and power,
It's then I know he's with me in every hour.
Jesus did it!

I feel his peace that passes all understanding
And know on any trip I'll have a safe landing...
Jesus did it!

When trouble's abound and I'm drowning in sorrow,
I know, in prayer, I'll have a better tomorrow...
Jesus did it!

I feel my hand in his holding me tight,
And I know with his help I'll win every fight...
Jesus did it!

He gave us life and will see us—till death.
This wonderful Creator who first gave us breath...
Jesus did it!

Grandma's Spice Box

My grandma had a spice box, eight drawers tall.
It held all the spices for cooking when I was small.
Later, when salt and pepper came in cans all their own,
Then she no longer used the spices she had grown.
But knowing grandma as a clever little fox,
I knew she would find a worthy purpose for that box.

When she passed away, I took it from its' familiar shelf.
Then with reverence, I slowly opened each little drawer myself.
With each precious find, how could I possibly have loved her more?
It's people like Grandma who will walk through heaven's door.
There was grandpa's wedding ring wrapped in tissue,
And next a birthday list for us all so no one could take issue.

The third drawer held a small cross with her confirmation verse.
My grandma saw her Creator throughout this whole universe.
One drawer is filled with all the small school pictures
In which toothless, silly grins are definite fixtures.
But she made over each and every one,
Making the presenter to feel like he just hit a home run!

A carefully wrapped item was in the next drawer space.
It was a fine white hanky edged in delicate lace,
And nestled inside it was a small pressed flower
From the day she married...what a blessed joyous hour!
Well, only three drawers left...can't imagine what it could be,
What Grandma has left behind for me to see.

And then, there it was...that little change purse
With the pennies...a reward for saying a Bible verse.
How could she know that I'd remember them to this day?
How they could bring me comfort in such a special way?
Almost to the end and here's the tiny ornament I made,
The little gold star from first grade...now suffering from fade.

It's the last drawer, Great-Grandma's thimble, she used to sew,
As stitches from busy hands just would seem to flow.
Now the silver is tarnished from the years that have passed.
How appropriate I should open this drawer last.
This brings our family full circle from all those years back.
Truly, for joy and love, our family never did lack.

Grandma preserved all these memories for us to one day treasure.
She somehow knew it would bring us great pleasure.
Just little pieces of the past kept in a spice box,
But think of the flood of memories that it unlocks.

PS: I forgot to mention what each drawer can still
share.
It's the pleasant aroma of sage floating in the air.

Life's Rhythm

Ever so slowly does our life change its pace,
And less often do we now present an eager face.
Fingers grow stiff and then refuse to work,
And have you noticed we sometimes walk with a little jerk?
A short stroll is about all I can now endure,
And often my next step is tentative...not so sure.

Those lovely stitches you once could sew,
The work that all your friends would know.
Even now when you sew with all your heart,
You find the stitches a little too far apart.
Our life's rhythm is slowing down quite a bit.
Now we watch a lot of life passing by as we sit.

No more walking to school or gardens with tomatoes to pick,
And sometimes our old memories don't come quite as quick.
But any worthy player tries to keep up with the beat,
Even if old age is something we all have to greet.
Reduce the tempo and just dance slow.
You have lovely memories from a long time ago.

My daily chores take a bit more time,
And stairs are getting a lot harder to climb.
But I'll reach my destination just the same,
Determination is often the name of the game.
All you youngsters remember when I sit and think,
I carry all my aged wisdom to its very brink.

Now I remember most of the paths once taken
And some of the efforts I left forsaken.
But we all still have our personal drummer,
He just marches slower in our winter than in our summer.
I'll do my best to keep life's rhythm going,
Even though I know my beat is slowing.

I'll march on until I can't hear my drummer anymore,
Then I'll just head home to that heavenly shore.

His Place

Today I seek but one thing... I search for inner peace
When I can say farewell to grief and give it release.
Then I'll walk taller with my head held high
Because I have a definite connection with the sky.

I can walk with my creator and feel his power,
And I look forward to his greatest hour.
When he comes here and takes us all home,
No more will this earthly place we roam.

I say it, yes, but understand it not so much,
But all it needs is just a bit of the master's touch.
After all, from dust we came...imagine that!
From a truly almighty hand we were beget.

Can't isn't a word he needs ever speak.
He who is always there to help the suffering and weak.
Like a father, he often pushes us along
When in our heart we just hear no song.

We feel lost, defeated, and want to quit.
We tell God that we just won't make it.
Then morning comes and the sun is shining.
Now we feel foolish doing all our whining.

Our shepherd leads his flock with mercy and grace.
Someday we'll all go home...oh, you know, to his place.

Good Night

It always seems to come...hidden somewhere deep,
Often arriving before I can find sweet sleep.
It gives me a hint, then a tug and a nudge.
There is no way I can ignore it and not budge.
The feeling is wonderful, beautiful, more than I can bear,
So I grip my pen and then try my best to share.
Like a hot bath or having dessert before my meal,
I just can't begin to explain how I really feel.

Special, yes, but I think I'd say blessed.
Each verse I sign is a challenge and a test.
God at my elbow cheering me on to write,
Giving me, at that moment, a special sight.
Tears often flow as the words roll out.
If my pen had a voice, I know it would shout.
It's then that the whole world changes...colors are brighter.
I love all humanity and wish to hold them tighter.

I'm thrilled with a light breeze and a bird's song.
Oh, surely, this world is good...it can't be all wrong.
See the beauty abounding around you everywhere...
Don' be afraid, your God made it all with great care.
He'll help you to climb every hill that comes your way,
And then finally take you home with him to stay.
This is what I see and how I feel every time,
When God gives my pen that little push to compose a rhyme.

Then I see without eyes and fly without benefit of wings,
And I can actually hear my soul as it sings.
What a great creation he made from just simple clay.
With that I'll close with "Good night,"...this is all I have
Left to say.

A Little Flower

Once I asked a flower what it really felt like to grow,
To just open your petals and let your beauty show.
To claim your colors and smile back at the sun,
And at that very moment to be with God as one.

That little velvet blossom with head lifted...smiled.
And I knew she was thinking of her life when a child.
A little bud struggling for strength...new to this old world.
Caught in life's storm...trapped in its cycle as she swirled.

Wind, rain, storms, and maybe even snow,
A threat to her life but she didn't know.
Then that hand reached down, that protects all the others.
All the trees and plants...you know, her brothers.

That scarred hand picked her up one day and helped her stand.
She could only say that the feeling was oh, so grand.
After our talk that day, I never pick flowers,
So I can enjoy their beauty and fragrance for hours and hours.

Grow where you're planted comes to mind,
And what a better example could you ever find
Than a little flower with her head held high,
Having a conversation with her father in the sky.

Touched From Above

Let the music play and play...loud and long.
At this moment, my soul needs to sing a song.
Bodily food is not my need... I crave melody's inspiration.
I want the core of me to have that perfect sensation
When man's heart and God's miracle meet.
When for an instant I am there...right there at his feet.

I feel his hand as he reaches for mine.
Then, just then, I know the meaning of divine.
I don't need life's breath to even live.
I have the power and strength that only God can give.
My feet no longer need to touch the ground.
This truly is a sacred dimension that I have found.

Just for an eye's blink, I see the world all spread out.
Only my voice is silent... I cannot shout.
'Tis not a sharing moment but mine to savor.
This taste of creation is such a scared and guarded flavor.
Perhaps once in a lifetime this precious experience is yours
And you are privileged to walk through one of God's holy doors.

Hold fast the moment, recall it with love...
The day Jesus reached out and touched you from above.

Once in Awhile

I want, for a moment, to feel like a child,
When my whole young life was simply family styled.
So at the dinner table I sat right there.
I had a little pillow to add height to my chair.

With my dad on the left and mom on my right,
This was my day in and day out kind of sight.
We table-talked about life and its living...
About other's troubles and our giving.

We prayed to open and close every meal.
I thought none of this as really a big deal.
But I learned some things as the years passed.
Childhood and its joys just do not last.

Days go faster...there's grief all around,
Often sneaking up on you without a sound.
Your joys are pulled in all directions,
And sorry but we don't make all the selections.

I like to remember popcorn balls and candy cotton,
But so many lovely things I have forgotten.
Sometimes I just take a whole lazy day,
And think of all that...be a kid that way.

I'm riding my bike with those balloon tires,
And wearing the pigtails that Grandma admires.
I recall school days and all the friends.
I never thought that a childhood ends.

With my old, dimming eyes I still see the past.
In my soul it will forever and ever last.
Every now and again, I'll look back and smile...
It's nice to return there once in awhile.

Rise Up

When the hills are steep and I'm worn out
And my voice so tired that I cannot shout...
I'll rise up.

Sickness may weaken, my family already frail,
But I won't let sadness be my personal tale.
I'll rise up.

I'll follow the sun and look to the stars.
I won't be stopped by any gate or bars.
I'll rise up.

I see the joy in all of life's choices,
And in my soul I hear the sweet, loving voices.
I'll rise up.

There is a plan for me... I have a story to tell.
I have a God who keeps saying, "All is well."
I'll rise up.

I feel the earth's energy holding me tight,
Always moving me forward into the light.
I'll rise up.

I'll cherish each moment with which I'm blessed,
And use my talents to meet each test.
I'll rise up.

Alone? No, never...never once since my birth.
Jesus is constantly reminding me that I have worth...
Together we always rise up!

Our Basket

We all carry a basket inside of us.
It can add to our life, a definite plus.
But only if we fill it with good common sense,
Then its' value proves to be immense.

Kindness toward others and honesty above all,
This kind of sense can help you stand tall.
As your basket of common sense fills to the top,
You will see that the benefits just never stop.

Use them daily...make all common sense your choice
And put those kinds of words into your voice.
We become people living a life of love,
Always guided by a power from above.

When our fellow man puts up a fence,
All we need do is use some of that common sense.
So let's keep that basket full and ready to go,
Common sense will always help your life to grow.

Mysterious Ways

A little bluebird flew too high one sunny day,
And went past the clouds far up and away.
There he was in this hushed and peaceful place,
But seeing no one there...not a single face.

Then he heard a voice...sounded like a child
Using simple phrases and speaking so sweet and mild.
It was a prayer for his mommy... "What could he do?
They said she's really sick and will go to heaven with you."

But our little man needed her. "With dad and me."
All his short life, there had always been those three.
"Could you please help her... Make me sick if you like
Or I just won't ask for that two-wheel bike."

Our little bird dropped a tear over that prayer.
Maybe there was some help that he could share.
Soon after this the mother saw with each morning sun
A little bluebird sitting in a tree...just one.

He sang a heartfelt message she didn't quite understand,
But nonetheless it cheered her...it sounded so grand.
It helped her feel stronger to challenge her days.
Our Father often works in these mysterious ways.

Forgotten People

Old, lost pictures...people gone from history.
All their living is now a complete mystery.
Their place in creation gone from all thought,
The people they loved...the battles they fought.

No one can recall a smile or their grin
Or know all of the places they have been.
Surely, there must have been those that cared,
And in their lifetime, they could have shared.

Time has a way of losing us as it passes by.
Hardly giving us a nod or pausing to sigh.
Forgotten people...just pictures in a frame.
Long ago separated from family, now with no name.

But still their voices will be heard once more,
When the family all meet on that other shore.
No need for pictures then...you will have the real thing.
A family reunion, as the bells of heaven ring.

Food for Thought

There are many subjects on which to feed.
Some are necessary, but for many we have no need.
Food for thought.

And it takes time to digest all that thought.
Often the moments spent are really worth naught.
Food for thought.

Of course, your mind is exercised…that's for sure,
Although personal reflections may be difficult to endure.
Food for thought.

When a subject isn't objective but rather close to home
Or perhaps when I'm composing yet another poem.
Food for thought.

When I walk deep into the crevices of my brain,
The majority of the food is mostly kinda plain.
Food for thought.

But now and again something extra special can't hurt.
So for my next thought, I'll treat myself to dessert!
Food for thought.

Henry

Henry was a cute little circus clown,
But sadly he always seemed to wear a frown.
When it was time for another tent show,
On would go his grin...he drew it on, you know.
So then he looked jolly for a little while,
But inside his tiny heart he carried no such smile.
Sad to say a pretend grin is never a very happy one.
Behind it, you never find any laughter or fun.

How many today walk around with a smile of paint?
People pretending to be what they really Ain't!
So busy painting they forgot who they are.
They can't remember the magic in a single star,
Or the peace to be found in a rainbow's beauty,
Or an owl perched in the tree all feathery and hooty.
People miss a lot of life when they are blue...
Oh, dear, don't tell me you're that way, too?

You and Henry need to throw all that paint away.
Then find a big mirror and sit in front of it all day.
Learn how to smile once again like the reflection you see.
Soon you'll do it all alone because you've set your soul free.

Children Grow Up

Chubby little creatures just bubbling with love.
How could they not be a gift from a Father above?
Into this world they came to its trouble and pain,
Lending yet another link to their family chain.
Dear innocent babies with so much to learn.
Right and wrong will all their life be a concern.
Every day is a challenge to do the right thing.
Never forgetting to hear all the birds that sing.

Guess you could say that I'm all grown up.
Really, no longer is there a need for a sippy cup.
Old would be the word to describe me best.
What a wonderful trip it's been…one joyous quest.

Unfortunately, it soon may be time for me to leave.
Please accept this little verse… 'tis truly what I believe!

We Can Never Tell

Poets jump out of windows when they create a rhyme.
They plunge into unknown space and distant time.
Feeling from their insides out, always with the heart,
Making its warmth and love what they impart.
Using long past memories to tell a cherished story
Or remembering, perhaps, a moment of personal glory.

We form words into phrases to reach the soul.
Always, this should be a writer's final goal.
Make the words draw emotion from the reader.
A well-written thought will always be a leader,
Showing men the way through the dark into light,
Often giving them the very will to stay and fight.

Gentle words can calm the turmoil of a troubled man
And often help him find an honorable plan.
Beautiful words will form an image in the mind.
A more attractive picture could be difficult to find.
Words, gentle or harsh or anything in between,
When well-written could maybe change a man's whole scene.

So I must think long and rhyme very well
Because who the reader might be, we can never tell.

Doubts

When I expressed some doubt, the Lord gave me a pen,
And I've been writing since I hardly remember when.
Whatever that problem was... I'm really not sure.
Absorbed in daily life, it became just a blur.

Prayers are never quite answered as we think they should.
Our Father will give us what is for our ultimate good.
Man is shortsighted...sees no longer than the end of his nose.
But Jesus observes life as far as the wind blows.

Now he quietly waits for us to find our knees
And drop to them, trying to find what he already sees.
He is patient...remember, it was from a cross he hung,
Forgiving his enemies with the last breath in his lung.

Oh, he gives you his hand so you can stand once more
And continue your onward trek to heaven's door.
Doubts will follow us all along our way.
It's good to keep in mind that we are just the clay.

The sculptor walks besides us all the time,
As now when I sit here and compose this rhyme.
I'll walk through many fields of doubt and fear.
But I'll always know that my comfort is so near.

He knows of all the places where doubt and fear lurk.
And remember, a good sculptor will always protect his work.

Remember When...

Lord, It's okay. I know I'll forget a lot by my life's end.
Maybe even how to give an old sock a good mend
Or a friend's name, an address, or something.
But, please, not the moment Vince gave me that ring
Or when I felt the first movement of our little girl.
She surely did keep our life in a joyous swirl.

Please allow me to remember those good times of my life...
Maybe I could just lose my thoughts of past strife.
Let me carry the feelings of love to my grave.
After all the years, Lord, love is really the only feeling to save.
Anger and envy are useless emotions...not to mention hate.
These become unnecessary as I approach God's gate.

My heart does well with loving thoughts of the past.
Such good, rich moments will always last.
They come forward when trouble grows strong,
When a turn in our life path has gone wrong.
So for this day, Lord...although I may forget which day it is,
I'm truly glad this talk isn't some kind of a quiz!

Today I'll give my soul a precious gift
And set my mind's recall on just drift.
I'll move in and out of the past as long as I can
And start a lot of my thoughts with "Remember when."

Any Other Way

Often the smallest kindness is the greatest gift.
The gentlest nudge proves to be the biggest lift.
A little smile sends the heart to a good place,
And a kind word puts a smile on a sad face.

We've all been there when our need was great.
When we just yearned for something...a counter to our hate.
Anger will prove nothing...it just ruins our day.
But sometimes we just can't see another way.

Then someone smiles and asks, "How are you?"
And you begin to feel a part of this blessed world, too!
You start to think that there may be another way.
Now a beautiful path is opening into your day.

Step on to it and walk ahead toward the sun.
You and the Father are beginning to become one.
Step by step, doubts and fear fall all apart.
Now, my friend, you're beginning to reason with your heart.

Oh, there will still be bumps...no path is entirely clear.
Once in awhile you may suffer a little fear.
But then you know how to clear the air.
Jesus gave us two hands that we can fold in prayer.

Now that's where you'll meet your ultimate friend.
He's the one that will see you through to the end.
We talk, he and I, every living day.
Neither one of us would have it any other way.

Smiles

Oh, please, don't cry...it can be catching.
Why not try a smile...it's ever so fetching.
A grin gives your eyes a special spark
And takes you to the light from out of the dark.

Your spirit lifts toward heaven's door,
Making any sadness much less of a chore.
Smiles are truly contagious, too...
They send happiness as they spread away from you.

I've never seen an angel with a frowny face.
A grimace is muslin...a smile is surely made of lace.
Always dress your face with a Sunday smile
And hold on to it as your everyday style.

Let the fabric of your life define who you are.
Smiling means you always have your eye on a star.
You will see this world as a much better place
When you wear a simple smile upon your face.

Along the Way

Be sure you get the measure of sunshine God made just for you,
And always keep your eye on your special star up in the blue.
Oh, sure, dark clouds pass over it every once in awhile
When your life faces a serious faith-robbing trial.
But it never leaves you...maybe you failed to look.
If that's the case, then you can always read his book.

You know the Bible...it's been around for ages and ages.
Literally, that long...you should read some of those pages.
Brave and faithful people struggling to live,
And Jesus showing us what life means when we learn to give.
He came to earth, you know, was a man like you.
And all of our same problems, he also went through.

In the end he died for us on a cross.
This whole world will never suffer a greater loss.
He overcame evil that gives man a problem all the time.
You really should read that book...not my pitiful rhyme.
You'll learn about his followers...twelve brave men.
In this book, Jesus saves them again and again.

He loved them so and he also loves each of us,
Even though we often sin and cause such a fuss.
Well, I've got to go and find my sunshine for today,
And maybe I'll get a glimpse of Jesus along the way.

Memories of Childhood

All red and white…a child's cupboard still in splendor,
Just needing a little help ever so tender.
Maybe a scrubbing and a bit of glue,
Just some loving care to make it as good as new.

Many children have opened those doors
And were very busy with their pretend chores.
A few dishes have surely been broken along the way,
But that's just part of a great day at play.

Grandpa made the cabinet when I was very small,
But it's still precious even after I've grown tall.
I helped him paint it all red and white.
When we were finished, I was quite a sight.

Red and white paint from my head to my toe,
What fun that was, you couldn't possibly know.
The shelves no longer hold Raggedy Ann dishes,
But only sweet memories of all my childhood wishes.

May your life be as long as the memories you share,
When you were just a happy child without a care.

Dessert

Music is the dessert of all the sound.
Relax and enjoy...you can't gain a pound.
Dance to it, sing, or just fall asleep.
Some sweet music, the mind will forever keep.

Sing a baby a lullaby or croon in a lover's ear
Or listen to notes that will bring a tear.
Be it man-made music or nature's own,
All is beautiful with its exclusive tone.

Memories are called forth with just a note or two,
Holding special past thoughts for only you.
Once heard, you'll hum them the whole day long.
Now that's when your dessert is truly a song.

Enjoy it, my friend...the music sweetly beckons.
Please feel free to indulge in seconds.

Grandma's Helper

All jobs done by one could be better done with two,
Especially when that other one happens to be you.
Every cookie baker needs someone ready to taste,
And a bowl licker that cuts way down on waste!

I'll always need a helper to fold laundry with me,
And talk about the kind of world she happens to see.
We might chat about Goliath or David with his sling,
Or maybe about Kool-Aid or Jelly Beans...just anything.

Maybe she'll take me back to my childhood long ago.
There is probably some lesson she should know.
Oh, what wonderful moments, more precious than gold,
Even makes you happy that you've become old.

They can learn from our experience, that's for sure,
But these youngsters give us a lesson in how to endure.
They bounce back from trouble wearing a smile
And they are always ready to walk that extra mile.

I'll take help from a little one any day of the week.
Maybe, with luck, I'll get a sweet kiss on my cheek.
It was, indeed, a wise man who said, "And a little child shall lead."
I believe it was that first gardener who planted a seed.

Gifts

All of our life, we are God-guided.
I didn't listen enough at times, I've decided.
I thought my ideas were better, I'd handle the situation.
My choice brought me something less than adulation.
First, I blamed others, then Him, then it was so clear.
The person to accept the fault is standing right here.

This child of God who knew better than anyone
What the problem was and what should be done.
When will I learn I'm not the shepherd but a sheep?
That's why each night I ask him my soul to keep.
Then that scarred hand reaches down and holds on to me,
As I struggle and thrash in his tossing sea.

He puts me back on shore so I can have another try.
I'll truly never be a star in his heavenly sky.
It's recorded that we are all made of clay.
Well, he formed me when he was having a bad day.
I always see his miracles, but after the fact.
There has to be something my clay lacked.

I often miss the wonder of a rainbow's glory
Or fail an opportunity to tell a sweet child a little story.
My arms could hug someone in need every day.
But often I forget to even see it that way.
And a smile...God made it so easy to do.
He just leaves the occasion up to you.

To see the artistry of a butterfly in flight
Or watch a world of fireflies in the evening light.
The tapestry of earth is gloriously made.
Created by a powerful God...made to never fade
But covers us all, shedding gifts galore.
Now how can a small sheep ever ask for more?

Little Messages

God sent me a message today by way of a bird.
It had the loveliest voice I've ever heard.
Oh, certainly, no words were exchanged at all,
But the message was clear from this courier so small.
With bright wings flashing in the morning sun,
He was going to give this day his very best run.
I felt his energy...his faith in life,
Telling me to rise above all my petty strife.
To cast my sorrows into the breeze,
And approach this day with confident ease.
To use my voice in a loving way,
And maybe be helpful with what I would say.
He'll fly the skies...as I walk the earth,
While God sees to it that we both have worth.
His eye is on that sparrow...that's very true,
And like every bird that flies his skies so blue.
He's been watching me, also, as I walk this earth...
From the very instant of my birth.
We often talk in this unconventional way,
And usually I know what he's trying to say.
There will be some sign in the course of my day
That tells me God is surely leading the way.
You have a great day... I know mine will be good.
I just got a little message... I knew that I would!

PS: The PS is rather long, but I think you will like it.

PS

Not fifteen minutes after I wrote this poem, I was sitting with Vince in the sunroom. I saw a fat gray dove walking on the deck table. Then this bird perched on the back of a patio chair not more than six inches away from the sunroom window right near where I was sitting. He looked right at me, twisting and turning his little fat neck for at least five to eight minutes. Even Vince was surprised at the attention I was getting, he thought maybe it was some reflection. I had brought little messages into the sunroom to read to him, as I do everything I write. When I finished reading the last line to him, we both just smiled. As I always say, "God is good!"

Eeny, Meany, Miney, and Moe

Please meet these four bears with no place to go.
Their lives hadn't stopped but were really getting slow.
No one to hold them and give a bear hug.
No fancy buttons or tags to help them feel smug.
They all ended up in this little house
And sat in a corner frequented by a small orphaned mouse.

They quickly became friends...three boys and one girl.
Around her small paw, these boys she could really twirl.
To them she was like a sister...their little gem.
She meant so much to the three of them.
They chatted endlessly day after day.
Occasionally, a child would visit and they would play.

They were Eeny, Meany, Miney, and Moe.
Miney preferred Minnie...a girl thing, you know!
In a group, they looked like sister and brothers,
But none of them actually shared mothers.
They were only related by way of the heart
And, of course, in a bear that's the very best part.

They shared endless stories about their life history.
Moe liked to exaggerate and always made his a mystery.
Minnie told of the sweet children she was parted from.
She secretly hoped they missed her and soon would come.
Eeny and Meany were the oldest of them all,
And knew that in life, one could often suffer a fall.

Meany was with a little boy that got sick and died
And his fur was soaked by all the tears that were cried.
Bears can't cry, but Meany's little heart was broken,
And for a long time after, he was silent...no words spoken.
Eeny's children were all grown and gone from the nest.
He remembered all the childhood times and liked them the best.

And so it is that as night falls on this little house,
Four small bears share a corner with a tiny, gray mouse.
They recall many good times and some bad, too.
Just like real people talk...remember, they hear you.
So next time you walk by that room, go kinda slow
And give a friendly nod to Eeny, Meany, Miney, and Moe.

Oliver Aardvark

Deep in the jungle Oliver Aardvark lived,
And his view of the world was quite negative.

He was sure mother nature had made an error
Because his looks brought nothing short of terror.

Here he was with a long funny nose
That clearly resembled a garden hose.

His ears were strange but his tail was worse.
He felt like the ugliest thing in the universe.

Having few friends...he came out just at night...
Thinking he was such a terrible sight.
His only two friends were a pair of mice.
Hearing of his sadness, they had some advice.

Way deep in the jungle they had heard of a place
Where you could get a message face-to-face.
Anyone who goes there is never the same,
But no one ever has given this a name.

The journey is said to be filled with fear...
Strange sights to see and things to hear!

Quickly, Oliver made a decision quite bold.
He was going to seek this story yet untold.
Going deep in the dark tangled brush
Where spiderwebs hung with a frightful hush.
Bats were screeching and swooped over his head.
Oliver's feet were now feeling like lead.
He began to sweat, though the air was chill,
But he pushed on with a force of will.

Branches reached down with skinny fingers...
This is not a place where someone lingers.
Oliver's legs went faster and faster,
On toward the answers from an unknown master.
A snake looped down and hissed in his ear.
Oh surely, his destination must be near.
Oliver wanted to turn and run from this place,
But he then would have his friends to face.

Suddenly there was thunder, lightning, a flash,
And Oliver tripped and fell with a crash!
Looking up, he saw a place of beauty with so much light.
After his dark journey, it was quite a sight.
Then through the shining mist, Oliver heard a voice
Calling his name...well, he had no choice.
He cleared his throat, and sounding like a frog,
Started his sad plight, settling down on a log.

Much time passed as Oliver bared his small soul.
Once started, he was on a definite roll.
Losing his fear, knowing this was a good place,
He had only to look at her loving face.
Who could she be...he didn't have a clue.
"I'm your guardian angel, Oliver, I watch over you."
Wow! Someone caring just for me.
I wish I wasn't so awfully ugly.
"Oh, Oliver, let me tell you a tale."
Our little friend held his breath and turned quite pale.

"Long ago, Oliver, the earth took a shower.
All was covered...every last flower.
One man, Noah, had a big boat,
And as the waters rose, it began to float.

"Noah and his family took many creatures, large and tall,
And a variety of the very small.
All went well until a giant wave
Tipped the boat...the results were grave.

"Waves were tossing the ark all about
When, suddenly, someone let out a shout.
For a few moments, fur was flying...
To say a minor event, I would be lying!

"As all the beasts were thrown to the right
And the small animals were lost out of sight,
With much grunting and struggling the group came apart,
And Noah knew it was his time to sort.

"For hours he separated all the little creatures,
Matching the parts to all of their features.
But, alas, at the end there were still some left on the floor.
Noah turned to God when he could do no more.

"'It's fine, my son, be of good cheer.
Your father will find a place for each little ear.

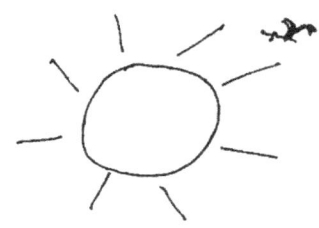

"Next morning the sun was shining bright,
And soon the waters took their flight.
Time to leave this special home
And find a place where they could roam.
Who led the parade when they left the ark?
Why one strange little animal called an Aardvark!
Special, you bet...he left by himself
Because God doesn't leave spare parts on the shelf!
A creation handcrafted by the Father above.
Using a double a name...now I call that love."

"Ugly, Oliver? Not in God's hand.
Like the lions and tigers that roam the land...
Made for a purpose only they can fill.
For your job, Oliver, you truly fit the bill."

On his way back from that special place,
Oliver wore a smiling, contented face.
He was loved and put together just right,
And God declared him perfect in his sight.

We, too, are formed with God's own hand.
And like Oliver, we don't always understand.
We need to find our angel and have a talk.
Like Oliver, she will help us on our life's walk.

About the Author

Grandma Moose, grew up in the historic town of St. Charles, Missouri where she still lives with her husband of sixty-three years. She is a mother, grandmother and great grandmother. Along with her husband, Vince, they run an auction business and have a home full of loving family memories.

CPSIA information can be obtained
at www.ICGtesting.com
Printed in the USA
JSHW030909241020
8931JS00006B/53